FACETED CLASSIFICATION

a guide to construction and use
of special schemes

Prepared by
B.C.VICKERY
for the Classification Research Group

Aslib

3 BELGRAVE SQUARE, LONDON, S.W.1
1960

SBN 85142 010 9

*Printed in Great Britain
by Photolithography;
Unwin Brothers Limited
Woking and London*

Contents

A   *Introduction*

The use of classification in libraries is traditional and its value is appreciated. For documentation and information retrieval in general, other techniques such as alphabetical indexing and machine selection are also available. That classification is of value in information retrieval as well as in book arrangement is, however, made evident in two ways. First, to achieve consistency and subtlety in alphabetical indexing and machine selection designers of such retrieval systems find the need to introduce classificatory techniques. Second, there is a continuing demand for the construction of special classifications for detailed arrangement and cataloguing of documents in restricted but intensively cultivated fields of knowledge.

It is to help meet these demands, particularly the second, that this guide has been prepared. The techniques of detailed depth classification have been greatly developed during the past decade, and instruments of much greater subtlety and efficiency than the traditional 'tree-of-knowledge' schemes can now be designed. These developments have been reported mainly as research papers in a variety of library journals and are often made unnecessarily difficult to follow by the use of unfamiliar terminology. There is a need for a more simply written and more readily available practical guide to the use of the newer techniques of classification.

THE CLASSIFICATION RESEARCH GROUP

The guide has been compiled for the Classification Research Group (CRG), which has been meeting in London since 1952 to discuss the principles and practice of classification unhampered by allegiance to any particular published scheme. The Group consists of about two dozen librarians, information officers, and others who are actively interested in documentation and indexing.

The Group's previous publications are a statement of aims and interim findings[1], 1953; a memorandum published by Unesco and the Library Association in 1955 on 'The need for a faceted classification as the basis of all methods of information retrieval'[2], and a bibliography of papers on classification and allied subjects by members of the Group[3], 1956. The CRG also helped to arrange and contributed to an International Study Conference on Classification for Information Retrieval held in 1957[4]. In connection with this conference, the Group produced three issues of a duplicated bulletin, reporting on its work, further issues of which appear in the *Journal of Documentation*[5]. As well as general discussions of classification, summed up largely in the above publications, the CRG has studied over a dozen special classification schemes prepared by its members. It is on all this material that I have drawn in compiling the guide. I must also acknowledge our debt to the work of S. R. Ranganathan[6].

A first draft of this guide was dissected in detail by the CRG and completely rewritten as a result. I am grateful to the following for their contributions to the discussion: Miss M. M. Armstrong, Mr D. V. Arnold, Mr T. I. Bell, Miss J. Binns, Miss D. Caldwell, Dr D. J. Campbell, Mr E. J. Coates, Mr R. A. Fairthorne, Mr J. E. L. Farradane, Mr D. J. Foskett, Mr J. F. Hadlow, Miss Barbara Kyle, Mr J. Mills, Mr R. Moss, Mr B. I. Palmer, Mr O. W. Pendleton, Miss J. D. Rollitt, Mr J. R. Sharp, Miss B. Warburton, Miss K. E. Watkins, Mr A. J. Wells, and Mrs M. Whitrow.

The technique of constructing a special faceted classification is not a settled, automatic, codified procedure. Nothing so complex as the field of knowledge could be analysed and organized by rule-of-thumb. We can therefore offer no more than a guide, describing tested procedures and discussing some difficulties. Despite its limitations, it is the hope of the CRG that the guide will be useful to those who find the need to devise new schemes for detailed subject cataloguing.

London, January 1960.   B.C.V.

B   *Why make a special classification?*

There are several published general classifications in existence: the Dewey decimal classification, the Universal Decimal Classification (UDC), the Library of Congress, Bliss, Colon classifications, and so on. Why not use one of these, rather than make a new special classification?

Several reasons may be given why existing general schemes are unsatisfactory. First, most of them do not give adequate detail for accurate specification of the highly complex subjects in papers and reports that documentation must handle today. Second, despite the comprehensiveness and variety of certain general schemes, they do not fully cater for the special viewpoints of each particular library or information centre. Third, even if they are varied in viewpoint, they do not sufficiently provide for the flexible combination of terms which highly specific subject headings demand. Fourth, even if flexible, they achieve such flexibility only by unnecessarily lengthy or complicated notational means. Fifth, they fail to give optimum helpfulness in filing order.

The continued proliferation of new special classifications is evidence enough that such criticisms are felt to be valid. It may be true that a general classification could be designed which would provide all the detail, variety, flexibility, and simplicity in use which modern information indexing requires. Until such a general scheme is provided new special classifications will be constructed.

On the other hand, any new general classification will lean heavily for its details on existing special classifications, provided that their general structure is based on principles similar to its own. This is an added reason why it will be helpful if new special schemes are designed on modern lines.

MODERN TRENDS IN CLASSIFICATION

The new style of classification developed in recent decades has become known by the names suggested by its main exponent, Ranganathan, viz. 'analytico-synthetic' or 'faceted'. The reasons why the old, enumerative tree-of-knowledge classification is being superseded are clear enough. The highly specific subjects catalogued today are *compound*: they can only be accurately designated by subject headings which combine two or more terms. Each term may be used in a great variety of combinations, so it is necessary to provide for complete flexibility of compound formation. Only in this way can *specific reference* to innumerable detailed subjects be provided. On the other hand, there is also a strong demand by users for comprehensive facilities in a file for *generic survey*: they want to be able to retrieve a document on a specific compound subject, not only when they look for that particular subject but also when they look for any term in the compound, or for any collective term embracing a term in the compound. This requires not only that terms be capable of unlimited combination but also that their generic or class relations be built into the system. Faceted classification is a device for achieving these results.

Its importance is made evident by its growing influence. First, there is its impact on the older general schemes. The UDC in its early days displayed some faceted structure. Schedules revised or newly developed during the last decade have been consciously constructed in this mould.[16] Second, there is the use of facet techniques in making special schemes, both in the United Kingdom, and increasingly in Europe. Third, its potential importance is suggested by the way in which non-conventional retrieval systems have developed. For coordinate indexing, the virtues of an unstructured, uncontrolled vocabulary of indexing terms were initially extolled, but as document collections grew the need for vocabulary control has been recognised. Facet analysis offers a set of principles and techniques for vocabulary control that have now been applied in a variety of subject fields. It is potentially of value to designers of retrieval systems of all kinds.

C *Faceted classification*

For a similar point

A faceted classification is a schedule of standard terms to be used in the subject description of documents. The terms are first of all grouped into homogeneous subject fields and a special classification may cover only one of these fields with the addition of some marginal material. Within each subject field the terms are divided into groups known as 'facets', and within each facet they may be arranged hierarchically. The facets are listed in the schedule in a prescribed order which is usually the order in which terms are to be combined to form compound subjects. By means of this combination order the relations between terms are displayed.

· As an example, we may look at a schedule for physico-chemical processes in pharmaceuticals manufacture. This field may be divided into ten facets, summarized below:

EXAMPLE

A. *Products.* The terms in this facet are drawn from basic schedules of substances, organisms, and organs, *e.g.*

gf	Acids		
gfk	Mineral acids		
lcb	Alcohols		
lce	Glycols		
m	Carbohydrates		
mg	Glycogen		
nb	Fatty acids	*Parts*	
x	Organisms	, b	Leaves
xd	Dicotyledons	, e	Flowers
xdro	Rosaceae	, f	Fruits
xdroc	Rosa	, h	Seeds
xdrok	Prunus	, k	Woods

y   Mammalian organs
yl   Liver
yp   Pancreas

B. *Starting materials*
C. *Substances to be extracted*
The terms in these two facets can be drawn from facet A.

D. *Reactions, e.g.*
  b Nitration
  c Sulphonation
  d Oxidation
  e Methylation

E. *Agents.* Terms to be drawn from facet A.

F. *Physico/chemical operations, e.g.*
  d Purification
  g Distillation
  ge   Fractional
  l Extraction

G. *Agents.* Terms to be drawn from facet A.

H. *Properties* of agents influencing action
  d Temperature
  h pH
  k Particle size

I. *Scale of operation*
  d Full production
  i Pilot plant
  l Laboratory
  n Micro

The provision of such definite facets helps the classifiers by providing a logical break-down of the subject. The classifier has only to decide which categories are represented in a document, and build up a class number for it on a prearranged plan. Categories are combined in a logical order, a category following one on which it is logically dependent. So we get combinations such as the following:

Fractional distillation of alcohols, Blcb Fge.
Extraction of fatty acids from Prunus leaves, Bxdrok, b Cnb Fl.

Oxidation of alcohols by mineral acids to give fatty acids, Anb Blcb Dd Egfk.

In the last example, the assignation of fatty acid, nb, to the products facet; of alcohols, lcb, to the starting materials facet; and of mineral acids, gfk, to the agents facet; makes clear the relations of these three substances in the compound subject.

As a second example, consider a schedule for Library Science, prepared by a subcommittee of the CRG[20]. There are four basic facets:

Library services (by persons receiving the service, by owner, by scope of service)
Library materials (by subject, by form)
Processes (technical, administrative)
Equipment

The combination of terms from different facets enables us to express subjects such as:

Professional duties in university libraries, Ui Fx
International classification research study conference, Hf Bj Bic
Initiating a mechanized union catalogue for medical libraries, Si 61 Lt Jtu Hmg
Putting the catalogue of a small company library into the KWIC index, Tg Hwg Hoe Em
Newspaper library reference collections, Tg Si07 Pi L

D   *The technique of facet analysis*

The essence of facet analysis is the sorting of terms in a given field of knowledge into homogeneous, mutually exclusive facets, each derived from the parent universe by a single characteristic of division. We may look upon these facets as groups of terms derived by taking each term and defining it, *per genus et differentiam*, with respect to its parent class.

Consider five terms in chemistry: 'alcohol' is a kind of chemical *substance*, 'liquid' is a *state* of that substance, 'volatility' a *property*, and 'combustion' a *reaction* of it, and 'analysis' is an *operation* performed by man on it. The five italicized words are the characteristics of division by which the terms are derived from the class, Chemistry. Looked at in another way, these characteristics are the logical *categories* by which the terms are assembled. From yet a third viewpoint, they express certain general *relations* between terms—*e.g.* the relation between 'alcohol' and 'combustion' is an instance of the general relation substance/reaction, and this relation might indeed be represented by a relational *operator* between the two terms.

NEW FEATURES

Facet analysis is therefore partly analogous to the traditional rules of logical division, on which classification has always been based. The result, however, differs from traditional classification in three ways. First, in the strictness with which the rules are applied: in the analysis performed in order to construct a scheme every distinctive logical category should be isolated, every new characteristic of division should be clearly formulated, every new relation should be recognized—even though at a later stage it may be possible and advisable to present a less refined analysis.

12

Second, a faceted classification differs from the traditional in that the facets so distinguished are not locked into rigid, enumerative schedules, but are left to combine with each other in the fullest freedom, so that every type of relation between terms and between subjects may be expressed. Third, from the theoretical point of view, faceted classification breaks free from the restriction of traditional classification to the hierarchical, genus-species relation: by combining terms in compound subjects it introduces new logical relations between them, thus better reflecting the complexity of knowledge.

Facet analysis, by means of fundamental distinguishing characteristics or *categories*, is the basic operation in constructing a faceted classification. As will be described below, the succeeding steps are: (*i*) to assign an order in which the facets will be used in constructing compound subject headings, (*ii*) to fit the schedules with a *notation* which permits the fully flexible combination of terms that is needed and which throws subjects into a preferred filing order, and (*iii*) to use the faceted scheme in such a way that both specific reference and the required degree of generic survey are possible. The whole sequence of operations will now be discussed in detail.

E *Choice of a subject field*

In deciding the field to be covered by a special classification, two problems have to be considered. First, what constitutes a homogeneous subject field and, second, can the needs of those who use the classification be served by a single homogeneous field, or is more than one field needed?

It is no easy task to state what is meant by a subject field. The titles of some classifications examined by the CRG may give some guidance: diamond technology, library science, enterprise activities, office management, food technology, social sciences. The general pattern of these subject fields is Thing-Process, Entity-Activity. In each case, a definite and definable group of things or entities (diamonds, libraries, enterprises, offices, foods, societies) is selected, and from the many relations in which they subsist (their properties, processes, operations, behaviour, activities) a certain number is selected as relevant. The selected activities may be the entire range associated with the entity (as perhaps in Office Management) or may be more limited (as in Food Technology, where the agricultural, nutritive, hygienic and gustatory aspects of food are excluded).

It is clear, therefore, that homogeneous subject fields of every size exist: we can limit our selection of entities from food to vegetables, or to a particular vegetable, say, beans; we can widen it to consumer products in general, or commodities in general. At each level of entity we can make a variety of selections as to which of its relations are to be included. Every such selection is a homogeneous subject field for a special classification.

Inhomogeneity arises if, instead of simply broadening the chosen group of entities, we select two or more entities which do not form a definable group. This may frequently be necessary if

14

the interests of users are to be fully met, as few groups of users are restricted to a single field of interest. A diamond technology classification, for example, finds it necessary to include not only the production and use of diamonds and diamond tools—a homogeneous field—but also the processing of hard materials in general. The special classification must include this subject field as well, either side by side with Diamond Technology as a second schedule, or subordinated to it in some convenient but perhaps arbitrary way. All special classifications, in fact, are faced with the problem of including marginal subjects.

F *Marginal subjects*

No special collection of literature, however narrowly selective, can hope to avoid the problem of marginal subjects. The average special library, serving the varied interests of its readers, will inevitably collect material on its own subject studied from marginal points of view, on tool subjects, and even on subjects quite distinct from its own which provide necessary background information.

For example, the central core of Diamond Technology includes (*i*) diamond production and cutting, and (*ii*) diamond tool production. Source materials for diamond production, production processes and equipment, diamond products and their properties, diamond tools, their production processes and equipment and their characteristics—these are all essential categories in the classification of Diamond Technology. But those working in this field are also interested in hard material processing in general, and a special classification for them must include such categories as non-diamond materials and worked objects and processes applied to them, non-diamond tools and products, their production and properties, technical measurements and scientific studies, and scientific instruments.

The practical problems faced by the classifier in a special field are: (*i*) how much marginal material should be included? (*ii*) how can it be integrated with the central core of the subject? and (*iii*) what provision can be made for drawing in other material as it is needed?

DRAWING IN MARGINAL MATERIAL

Marginal subjects comprise terms and categories which may be central in some other classification. It is reasonable to suggest

16

that if other classifications are available, special or general, in which the needed marginal subjects are adequately analysed and scheduled, then they need not be repeated (except perhaps for convenience of reference) in the classification under construction. For example, in a classification for Enterprise Activities, the primary facet is the *kind* of enterprise, and it may be directed that terms for this facet can be drawn direct from the standard industrial classification. A similar directive may be given with regard to the Industries facet in insurance. At many points in the Colon classification, chemical substance terms are thus drawn into another subject field from the *matter* facet in chemistry.

Using another classification scheme in this way needs a suitable *intercalation* device in the notation, as will be discussed later, but it may also have disadvantages. The terms in the extraneous schedule may not be listed in a helpful order—in particular, frequently occurring marginal terms may be buried in a series of rarely occurring ones. The solution in this case is to list—in the appropriate facet of our special classification—the most important *favoured* terms, and to direct that other terms be drawn in from the extraneous schedule as required.

EXAMPLE

Soil constituents
  Chemical
    Inorganic
      Mineral reserve ⎫
      Nutrient
      Trace elements
      Silica/sesquioxide ratio
      Nitrogen   ⎬ Favoured terms
        Ammonia
        Nitrite
        Nitrate
      Phosphorus ⎭
      Other (subdivide by chemical substance schedule in UDC, Colon, or Bliss)

17

Soil properties
  Physical
    Mechanical composition ⎫
    Degree of aggregation   ⎪
    Cohesion
    Consistence
    Plasticity   ⎬Favoured terms
    Permeability
    Porosity
      Capillary
      Non-capillary   ⎭
    Other (subdivide by physical properties in UDC, Colon, or
      Bliss)

If the number of such favoured terms is small, and other terms are very rarely needed, the favoured schedule can simply be used as it stands, with no reference to the fuller schedule of another classification. If required, provision can be made to add new terms at the appropriate position alphabetically.

PROVIDING SCHEDULES

It may well be the case that no suitable extraneous schedules are available for a related marginal subject, and then it too will have to be analysed and scheduled. This has been done in the Diamond Technology classification mentioned earlier, which contains three groups of facets: (*i*) those specific to Diamond Technology, (*ii*) those concerned with objects and materials on which diamond tools are used, and (*iii*) those relating to non-diamond tools, materials and products which are also used in Hard Materials Processing.

A particularly frequent type of marginal subject is the 'tool' subject which is used in the experimental or theoretical study of the core—*e.g.* Electronics, Photography, Mathematics. These are often more or less independent of the central subject, and background material on them is collected. It is not easy to decide where such material may most usefully be placed in the classified catalogue. In a general classification, it would be classed quite separately from the core subject. This practice is followed in an

18

Office Management classification, which includes in a common facet the heading 'Tools and aids in applying the subject'. In Diamond Technology, marginal Non-technical Processes (Prospecting, Packaging, etc.) are placed in a separate auxiliary schedule.

An alternative procedure is followed in an Insurance classification. Here, a background reference on, say, Textile Industries, is placed with that section of Insurance which has most to do with Textiles—in this case, with 'Fire insurance: textile industry'—since it is the reader in this last subject who most often needs such background information. Such a collocation is helpful only (*i*) if reader needs are clear, and (*ii*) if the background subject remains a minor interest. As soon as it grows large—or as soon as the associations of Textiles with Insurance become more varied—such special collocation may become unhelpful, and the marginal subject should then be listed in an independent facet.

An example of providing an extended set of marginal schedules —amounting to half the total scheme—comes from the CRG classification for Library Science.[20] In addition to the core facets, noted on page 11, schedules are provided for:

Organization and management
Knowledge and learning
Education
Research
Museums
Authorship
Reading
Writing
Bibliography
Paper
Documentary reproduction
Bookbinding
Publishing
Bookselling
Non-book, non-printed materials

19

G   *Formulation of categories and facets*

Having defined a homogeneous field of specialization, the core of a special classification, the first step is to analyse it into facets. This can be achieved only by a detailed examination of the literature of the field to be classified. It is useful to study systematically organized textbooks, in which the general structure of the field is apparent. Glossaries aid in the more refined formulation of categories by means of definition with respect to their parent class. The examination of a collection of specific subjects—*e.g.* in an abstracts journal in the field—brings to light the more detailed structure of the subject.

Facet analysis is essentially a conceptual analysis of the subject matter, but basing it upon the literature ensures that the characteristics of division isolated are those which actually give rise to literature and are significant in the study and practice of the subject. The theoretically unlimited number of characteristics by which a subject could be divided is thus restricted to those which are relevant to the work in hand—cataloguing documents.

ISOLATING CATEGORIES

An example of the way in which one particular analysis was carried out may be useful, although it is not offered as the only possible method of approach. To analyse Soil Science, a representative collection of terms was first examined—a glossary of over 350 terms. Each term was assigned to a provisional category which its definition suggested. Specimen terms, their definitions and assigned categories, are given below.

cohesion: the property of particles sticking together to form an aggregate. *Property.*

gravel: particles between 20 and 2 mm. in diameter. *Part* of soil.

20

sticky point: maximum moisture content at which kneaded soil
ceases to stick to a knife. *Measure* of soil property.

muck: partially decomposed organic matter. *Parent material*
of soil.

mineralization: release of mineral matter from organic combination. *Process* occurring in soil.

amendment: work making soil more productive. *Operation* on
soil.

Proceeding in this way, fourteen categories were isolated:

Category	Example
Soil, according to constitution	Peat soil
Soil, according to origin	Granitic soil
Soil, according to physiography	Desert soil
Physical part of soil	Gravel
Chemical constituent of soil	Nitrogen
Structure of soil	Profile
Layer of soil	Horizon
Organism in soil	Bacteria
Parent material of soil	Muck
Process in soil	Mineralization
Property of soil	Cohesion
Measure of property	Sticky point
Operation on soil	Amendment
Equipment for operation	Plough

A study of existing classifications of Soil Science suggested four
new categories:

Soils, according to texture	Sandy clay
Soils, according to climate	Arctic soil
Substances used in amendment	Lime
Operations on these substances	Placement

These eighteen groups of terms became the provisional facets of
the classification.

HIERARCHIES IN THE SOILS FACET

It will be noticed that there are five Soil facets—according to
constitution, origin, physiography, texture, and climate. Soils,
which might be considered as a single facet, are thus cross-

classified into five hierarchies, each of which is treated as a single facet. The different hierarchies are virtually independent. A given term—in this example, a given kind of soil, *e.g.* laterite, desert, solonets, sand—is by literary warrant always placed in a particular hierarchy. Even though a desert soil may in fact be sand, the two terms are used in different contexts and there is no confusion as to the hierarchy a given term should be assigned to. This situation is most likely to arise in subject fields where the grouping of terms is still largely conventional, and not based on close scientific analysis. An extract from the Soils schedule is given below.

Soils by origin (subdivide by Rock schedule)

Soils by climate	Soils by physiography
Arctic	Desert
Temperate	Prairie
Subtropical and tropical	Forest
Laterite	Rain-forest
Red earth	Swamp
Red loam	Lake
Terra rossa	Soils by constitution
Regur	Allitic
Humid	Siallitic
Arid	Pedalfers
Chernozem	Pedocals
Smonitza	Peat soils
etc.	Podzols
Soils by texture	Gley
Sand	Saline and alkaline
Loam	Solonchak
Clay	etc.
etc.	

H *Fundamental categories*

The process of recognizing and distinguishing the categories in a subject almost inevitably raises the question of whether such facet analysis could be facilitated by the prior recognition of a limited number of fundamental categories. For example, it is well known that Ranganathan postulates that there are only five such categories, which he calls personality, matter, energy, space, and time. Of these, Space and Time are the relatively straightforward geographical and chronological schedules. Energy covers categories such as problem, method, process, operation, handling, and technique. Matter comprises constituent materials of all kinds. Personalities include libraries, numbers, equations, wavelengths of radiation, engineering works, organisms, crops, religions, art styles, literary works, languages, social groups, communities, and states. The two major categories of Personality and Energy recall the useful indexing distinction between Concretes and Processes made by Kaiser many years ago. Despite the generality and vagueness of these terms, more precise categories can often be assimilated to them to a surprising extent, as a study of Ranganathan's use of them will show.

For the field of science and technology, a longer list of fundamental categories has proved helpful: substance (product), organ, constituent, structure, shape, property, object of action (patient, raw material), action, operation, process, agent, space, and time. As well as these, in any scientific classification there may occur a number of terms applicable at several points in the combination formula. For example, any property or process may itself have a general property: rate, variation, and so on. There are general operations on properties (*e.g.* measurement) and on processes (*e.g.* initiation, control). There are also a number of

23

operations connected with apparatus (equipment, instruments) such as design and maintenance. Lastly there are a number of common logical or mental operations: comparison, explanation and so on.

Other lists of fundamental categories have been proposed, showing considerable similarity to the above. Shera and Egan, for example, suggest the categories of agent, act, tools, object of action, time, space, and product. Barbara Kyle has written of natural phenomena, artefacts, activities, and 'purposes, aims, ideas, and abstracts'. De Grolier suggests the 'constant categories' of time, space, and action, and the 'variables', substance, organ, analytic, synthetic, property, form, and organization.

USE OF A FUNDAMENTAL LIST

Any such list of fundamental categories should not be used mechanically and imposed upon the subject, but to use it as a provisional guide in approaching a new field can be helpful. It provides an outline framework which may fit the field, and give guidance in suggesting possible characteristics which should not be overlooked. On the other hand, it must never be taken to exhaust the field, nor to be necessarily applicable in all subjects. The following examples illustrate categories actually used in some special classifications.

EXAMPLES

Occupational safety and health
  Industries
  Special categories of worker
  Sources of hazards
  Industrial diseases
  Preventive measures
  Organization and administration
  Occupational pathology
Insurance
  Branch of insurance
  Property insured
  Persons insured
    according to industry
    according to other characteristic

Risk insured against
Insurance operations
Insurance organization
Office management
  Kinds of office
  Services and procedures
  Accommodation, equipment, supplies
  Personnel
  Organization, control, finance
Enterprise activities
  Aim or kind of enterprise
  Size of enterprise
  Personnel activities
  Supply, production, marketing, and public relations activities
  Ownership, trusteeship, general, financial, office and its activities
  Management activities and general techniques
Social sciences
  People, population
  Psychological make-up and sex relations
  Community, society
  Government, formal organization
  Productive, distributive, and consumptive activities
  Law
  Communication
  Arts and crafts, culture
  Values, aims, opinions, attitudes, motivations, states, conditions
  Ideologies
  Environment, physical and economic
  Geographical location
Music literature
  Composer
  Executant
  Form of composition
  Elements of music
  Character of composition
  Technique

25

Food technology
   Products
   Parts
   Materials
   Operations
Container manufacture and packaging
   Products
   Parts, components
   Materials
   Operation of manufacture
   Machinery for manufacture
   Machinery for processing
   Packs
   Processing of packs

I   *Combination order of facets*

The order in which facets are combined in building up a compound subject heading is of great consequence in a classified catalogue. In the first place, combination order determines the sequence of terms which describe the subject, and it is helpful if this sequence (and index entries derived from it) should be readily understandable by the user. For example, the following heading used to represent a complex subject is reasonably comprehensible, as is its reversed index entry:

Rat: tissue: noradrenaline: concentration: variation: seasonal

Seasonal variation: concentration: noradrenaline: tissue: rat

whereas other sequences might not be so helpful.

EFFECT OF COMBINATION ORDER ON GROUPING

A more important consequence of the chosen combination order is that it determines how headings will be grouped in the file. If we have facets A, B, C, D . . ., and a series of headings compounded from terms in these facets, how do we wish the references to be arranged? For example, in a classification of Enterprise Activities, do we want the first broad grouping to be by kind of enterprise (subdivided by activity) or by kind of activity (subdivided by enterprise)? In Food Technology, should the primary division be by products or operations?

A decision to group, say, by products rather than by operations implies that products are more significant as a first approach than operations in the study of food technology. This significance is confirmed by the fact that most textbooks are divided up by food product. The relationship between different operations on a particular product is considered more significant to the users of the classification than the affinities between the same operation

27

applied to various products. Such a grouping means that references are gathered together at the various groups of foodstuffs, and this is in fact the way the industry usually works, rather than according to operations. It appears at first sight that there are exceptions such as 'canners', who are food processors practising food sterilization by heat, and whose primary interest would therefore seem to be in the process. But a closer look at the industry shows that there is in fact a considerable degree of specialization according to food group. Fruit and vegetable canners, meat canners, fish canners—these are the main groups, and only the largest firms actually go in for more than one group. So the most generally helpful arrangement in this case would be one in which product comes before operation in the combination order.

CHOICE OF COMBINATION ORDER

It might be argued that the empirical study of helpfulness to users should decide the whole sequence of facets used in compound headings. We should collect data on the grouping of subjects in the literature and on the approach of catalogue users. Since the collected evidence is likely to be conflicting, the most generally helpful combination order may have to be decided statistically, or arrangements made for alternative orders in different circumstances. However, the systematic collection of such data for subjects containing a number of categories is a long and difficult task, impracticable though not impossible. An instinctive and empirical knowledge of helpful combination order is developed by literature searchers and catalogue makers in the course of their work, and it is on this instinct, this 'feel' for a subject, or 'flair', that the choice of order must often rely.

Attempts to codify and hence transmit this instinctive knowledge from experienced to less experienced classifiers take the form of suggested principles of combination order, or of standard formulae proposed for named categories. Ranganathan has put forward the principle of 'decreasing concreteness'—categories of more concrete concepts should be cited before those of less concrete concepts. Thus, in Agriculture, crop is the primary category, more concrete than the farming operations and problems which follow it. In the Social Sciences, people and communities are more concrete than their activities. This criterion of concreteness is not always easy to apply, and is not in itself sufficient. For example, in the subject already quoted in this section, which is more concrete, rat, tissue, or noradrenaline? Concentration or variation?

A second principle which has been advocated is that of purpose or use. For example, in any technology the end product (which is the very *raison d'être* of the subject) should precede the processes and operations contributing to it. The growing of a particular crop is the object of farming, so 'crop' is the primary category in Agriculture. The provision of library service is the object of Librarianship, so the library service—exemplified in particular kinds of library—is prior in this field. This criterion is capable of rather wider application than that of concreteness. With any two categories A and B, if on analysis we find that A is the object, the action, or the end towards which B is directed, we can take it to be of prior importance in grouping references and hence earlier in combination order.

GENERAL COMBINATION FORMULA

Such principles as the above can be used to order a particular set of facets which have been obtained by analysis of a particular subject. They can also be used to suggest a general combination formula for a set of fundamental categories, applicable to all subjects. Thus Ranganathan lists his fundamental categories in the following order of decreasing concreteness: personality, matter, energy, space, and time. He would assign the terms in the subject 'Manufacture of woollen gloves in Bradford in the nineteenth century' to the following categories, combined in the order shown:

Gloves : woollen : manufacture : Bradford : nineteenth c.
Personality   Matter   Energy   Space   Time

Similarly, the fundamental categories suggested earlier for science and technology may be ordered by the principle of purpose. The parts, constituents, and properties of a substance are dependent on that substance, which forms the central idea to which the other categories contribute. For example, the chemical constituents of soil, *qua* constituents, are only of interest for the light they throw on soil as a whole. Operations such as ploughing are directed towards affecting the state of the soil, and the purpose of a tool such as a plough is to carry out the operation for which it is used. Again, the measure of a property is directed towards that property. The principle of purpose thus suggests two combination chains: (*i*) substance/part/constituent/property/measure, (*ii*) substance/action, operation or process/agent or tool. Combining such chains gives the following suggested combination order (the letters are added for ease of reference):

P: Substance, product, organism
O: Part, organ, structure
C: Constituent
Q: Property and measure
R: Object of action, raw material
E: Action, operation, process, behaviour
A: Agent, tool
G: General property, process, operation
S, T: Space and time

Examples of the application of this formula are provided by the following subjects (the categories to which terms have been assigned are bracketed):

1. Occurrence of caesium in fossils.
   Fossils (P): caesium (C): occurrence (E).
2. Osmotic pressure in cow intestine.
   Cow (P): intestine (O): osmotic pressure (Q).
3. Polyhedroses of insect cells.
   Insect (P): cell (O): polyhedrose (C).
4. Experimental infection of turkey with Eimeria.
   Turkey (P): infection (E): Eimeria (A).
5. Bacterial fermentation of sugar to give methane.
   Methane (P): sugar (R): fermentation (E): bacteria (A).
6. Seasonal variation of noradrenaline concentration in rat tissue
   Rat (P): tissue (O): noradrenaline (C): concentration (Q): variation, seasonal (G).

This last example shows how the *part*, tissue, and *constituent*, noradrenaline, are cited later than the equally concrete *organism*, rat; and the *general* process, variation, later than the particular *property*, concentration.

Despite the utility of general combination formulae, it is unwise to rely entirely on them, however well tested they may appear to be. In a special classification designed for specialist users, it is their interests which are paramount. In a catalogue serving process engineers in an industry, it may well be that the primary category should be operations, not products. To the biochemist, it may be that the chemical constituents and processes of a living organism are a more helpful basis of primary grouping than the organisms in which they occur. Only sensitive attunement to the literary needs of his users can provide the specialist classifier with an answer to such problems.

J   *Schedule order of facets*

Considerations such as those just outlined will have provided,
first, a set of facets making up the field of a special classification,
and second, a preferred order for combining these facets in
compound subjects. The facets must be written down in the
classification schedule in a certain sequence, and the simplest
schedule order to adopt is the combination order. The categories
in the sample classifications of section H are listed in this order,
i.e. in Food Technology, 'products, parts, materials, operations'
is both combination and schedule order. Some special classifications make schedule order the reverse of combination order,
following the practice of Ranganathan, for reasons which have
been argued by J. Mills[4].

It sometimes appears convenient, however, to modify the basic
combination order when scheduling facets. For example, in a
classification of Occupational Safety, we find each term in a
category *parts of the body* (respiratory system, skin, etc.) immediately followed by terms from a second category, the *diseases* of
that part:

De	Respiratory system
Deb	Asthma
Dem	Bronchitis
Deq	Pneumonia
Des	Silicosis, etc.
Df	Circulatory system
Dfg	Anaemia and leukaemia, etc.
Dj	Skin
Djb	Eczema
Djc	Allergic dermatitis

DIFFERENTIAL FACETS

The result of this arrangement is that one of the categories is split up. Instead of a complete Disease facet following a complete Parts facet, different diseases are allocated to different terms in the Parts category. The need for this arises when each of the terms in a given facet M may require to be followed by a different set of terms in the facet N which immediately succeeds it in combination order.

For example, in Library Science, the processes applicable to maps (in the Materials category) may differ considerably from those applicable to periodicals. Again, in Food Technology, the processes applicable to the product cereals are, in the main, different from those applied to meat or fruit and vegetables. While the actual category (Processes) is common to all the products, the terms in it vary to a large extent with the terms in the Products category. In such a case, instead of listing all the processes together, the category may be split into differential facets.

The use of differential facets is highly developed in the Colon classification schedules for Medicine and Agriculture. In the latter, for example, each of the seven terms in the Energy (or farming) facet has its own chain of differential facets: *e.g.* Disease is followed by *agent* and *problem*, Manuring by *substance* and *operation*, Harvesting by *operation*. The problems and operations are all 'second-round energy' category, but this category is separated into seven differential facets, as in the following example. The names of the facets are italicized, with terms in them which lead to differential facets.

EXAMPLE

Crop
Farming
  Soil
    Kinds of soil
    Operations, including
      Amendment
        Materials (*e.g.* lime)

33

Manure
  Kinds of manure
    Operation (*e.g.* placement)
Propagation
  Part of plant
    Operation (*e.g.* grafting)
Disease
  Agent
    Operation (*e.g.* pathology)
Development
    Operation (*e.g.* pruning)
Harvesting
  Part of plant
    Operation (*e.g.* gathering)

The Operations category is thus distributed into half a dozen differential facets.

COMMON FACETS

On the other hand there are cases where, although the terms in the secondary facets are largely different, there are some common terms. If the whole category is kept together in a single facet these common terms need be listed once only. Further, in Food Technology for example, there are some operations which, though different for each product, can be described in a sufficiently general way to fit several products, *e.g.* the 'removal of non-edible portions' (such as husk, chaff, peel, core, bone).

An advantage of keeping a category in a single common facet is that it is always possible that one term in it—say, an operation—used for one product only, may in due course be applied to another, and is thus already available in the scheme for use. In Container Manufacture, the raw materials included metal and paper, and the operations included drawing, a process applied to metals. When later drawing was applied to paper, the existing single operations facet supplied the term, and no addition to the schedule was necessary.

One advantage of differential facets is that, each comprising only a small number of terms, notational symbols may be shortened. A decision whether to use differential or common facets should take this point into consideration.

The effect of using them, however, is to complicate the schedule order. Although the facets are still combined in the order in which they appear in the schedule, the simple listing of categories in sequence is lost, as is shown by the above summary of the Colon schedule for Agriculture.

The same is true in an Aeronautics classification. The facets in this subject can be put into six fundamental categories:

> *things* (kinds of aircraft)
> *parts, components* (of aircraft structure)
> *materials* (of construction)
> *properties, behaviour* (of aircraft, of components, of materials)
> *operations* (of aircraft, of manufacture, of test)
> *operating agents* (instruments, tools)

However, the general arrangement in this sequence is considerably modified because of complex relations between facets. At various points in the schedule, the basic sequence is interrupted to insert a differential facet, for example: (1) in the facet, Parts of aircraft structure, the groups Rotors and propellers is followed by a new facet listing Parts of rotors and propellers; and the term Fuselage is similarly followed by a Parts facet; (2) in the facet, Properties of materials, the group Mechanical vibrations is followed by a facet listing Properties and processes relevant to vibrations. The placing of a differential facet immediately after the group of terms it qualifies leads to the insertion of *property* and *agent* facets at many points in the schedule.

K *Common subdivisions and relational terms*

Three types of common subdivision are usually required in a special classification—geographical (space) and chronological (time) subdivisions, and form subdivisions. The geographical and chronological subdivisions can often be drawn from some published general scheme. Sometimes, however, the places and periods of interest are quite restricted and it may be more convenient to compile special schedules.

The bibliographical or literary form divisions may vary greatly according to the subject field of the classification—each subject having its own forms of literature. Some forms found useful in classifications examined by the CRG are shown in the following schedule.

Archive
Serial
Bibliography, catalogue
Glossary
Encyclopaedia
Law, code, statute
Patent
Specification, standard
Trade catalogue
Table
Conference proceedings
Graph
Letter
Cutting
Exhibition catalogue
Advertisement

Directory
Collection
    Abstracts
Thesis, dissertation
Report
Yearbook
Imaginative work
Diagram, plan
Physical form
    Pamphlet
    Book
Manuscript
Printed
Duplicated
Photocopied
    Microcopied

It is also often convenient to include as common subdivisions such common marginal subjects as history, biography, law, statistics.

RELATIONAL TERMS

As has already been explained, the combination of terms from two categories in a faceted classification implies the existence of a relation between them. However, apart from such implied relations, it is useful to have available a number of explicit relational terms which can be used to link other scheduled terms.

One of the most commonly needed is the influencing or *effect* relation, as in 'the effect of physical structure on the engineering properties of plastics'. The relation of *comparison* is also quite common. Often there is an *association* established between two terms, without any more particular relation being specified, as in 'growth *and* sexual maturity in aquatic mammals'. The 'bias' relation exists when one subject is studied from the point of view of another, *e.g.* 'statistics for economics' and 'physiological anatomy' (= anatomy from the viewpoint of physiology).

L   *Contents of each facet*

When categories have been set up for a subject field, the next step is to enumerate the contents of each facet as far as possible. The advice of subject experts is useful here, but the task can also be carried out by using standard reference works, glossaries, indexes, abstracts, and so on. This stage of the work is, more than any other, based on literary warrant.

It must be remembered that the task is never completed—new discoveries and hence new terms will occur unceasingly—so that the classifier can never produce a complete schedule. He must be as complete as the literature allows, and must ensure that his schedules provide a place for all the additional terms which will arise. This involves not only providing room for each new term, so that it can be added in the future, but also ensuring that a helpful position for the new term relative to the others can be allotted. These are notational problems which will be discussed later.

HIERARCHICAL ARRANGEMENT

Terms having been assembled in each facet, they may now be arranged hierarchically. This is the established technique of traditional classification, and its principles have often been described.

Terms are subordinated one to another, the whole assembly being organized into the familiar 'tree of knowledge', with the category itself forming the origin or *summum genus*. It is differentiated into a set of subclasses, using a *characteristic* of division. Such characteristics should be chosen for their relevance to the purpose of the classification, their ascertainability, and their

38

relative permanence. The subclasses derived from a parent class by application of a single characteristic form an *array*, and should as far as possible be mutually exclusive.

Each subclass is itself subdivided into a further array by the application of another characteristic. A series of subordinated classes is called a *chain*. The sequence of terms in a chain depends upon the sequence in which successive characteristics of division are applied. This can only be chosen for its relevance to the purpose of the classification, so that documents are collected on that aspect of a subject which is most important to the user.

ORDER IN ARRAY

An array consists of a series of subclasses derived from a parent class by application of a single characteristic. Is order in array of any importance? If the references under a particular term in an array do not satisfy the user, are references under collateral terms —allegedly mutually exclusive of the sought term—likely to be of aid? The possibility that they may be arises from the fact that the terms, even though mutually exclusive, may be similar in varying degree, so that information on, say, a Society library may be of some use to a reader seeking Research institution library—more use than information on Public library, which is a more remote class in the same array. The likelihood that this will be so is increased by the fact that documents are rarely as mutually exclusive as the headings by which we locate them, and may often refer in passing to closely related subjects.

Consequently, although order in array may be of less importance than other aspects of file order, it should not be neglected. Various principles of order have been suggested by E. C. Richardson and S. R. Ranganathan and are worth remembering: (*i*) from simple to complex, or the reverse; (*ii*) spatial or geometrical; (*iii*) chronological, or historical, or evolutionary. Chronological order is a ubiquitous and exceptionally helpful principle; it is not only important in historical studies, but in arranging the processes and operations in any technology. Some examples of these three orders follow.

EXAMPLES

From simple to complex
  Elements of language
    Phoneme (vowel, consonant)
    Syllable
    Word
    Phrase
    Clause
    Sentence
    Paragraph
    Composition
Spatial
  Planets (relative to Sun)
  · Mercury
    Venus
    Mars
    Asteroids
    Jupiter
    Saturn
    Uranus
    Neptune
    Trans-Neptunian
Chronological
  Food technology, preliminary operations
    Transport
    Delivery, unloading
    Sorting, grading
    Trimming, peeling
    Seeding, stoning, coring
    Cleaning, washing
    Blanching
    Cutting, slicing
    Filling into containers
    Closing containers

ALPHABETICAL ORDER

On the other hand, it often happens that, while the terms in an array are all derived from the same parent class, they do not bear

40

any relation one to another that would enable us to say that one should precede or follow another. As 'sources of hazards' in Occupational Safety we have terms such as fire, industrial equipment, electricity, dangerous radiations. It seems reasonable to keep electricity and dangerous radiations together, but apart from these the sequence has no particular significance or helpfulness.

In such cases one may adopt a conventional sequence which has literary warrant. However, literary warrant for order in array is rarely clear cut and is constantly changing. The value of ordering by some principle—even if it is of no great significance—is that later additions to the array can be interpolated helpfully.

Even more unequivocal aid in interpolation is offered by the ordering of such 'unprincipled' arrays alphabetically. Wherever there is no preferred sequence, alphabetical order in array can be adopted—and it has the added advantage of requiring no added notation to preserve the order in some situations.

M   *Cross-classification within a facet*

Cross-classification arises when a group of terms is of interest to users from a number of viewpoints, so that several of its attributes are used as characteristics of division. A typical example of this is the category of Industrial Chemicals. This may be divided by the characteristics of elementary constitution (fluorine compounds), functional group (benzene derivatives), structural type (polymers), chemical behaviour (acids), physical behaviour (elastomers), biological behaviour (enzymes), use (abrasives, dyes), origin (petroleum chemicals), physical state (colloids), mode of production (fermentation products), scale of production (heavy chemicals), etc. Each characteristic gives rise to a separate hierarchy.

A similar situation has been discussed in connection with Soils, on page 22, but in the present case there is confusion as to the hierarchy to which a given term belongs. Sulphuric acid, for example, is an acid, a petroleum chemical, and a sulphur compound; some enzymes are fermentation products; aniline is a nitrogen compound, a benzene derivative, a base, a dye intermediate, and so on. In the early days of chemical industry, no doubt, a given product was conventionally assigned to a particular hierarchy, based on the traditional grouping of manufactures in industrial establishments. Today, when chemicals are made by a variety of processes and have many uses, they can figure in several hierarchies.

SOLUTIONS

Three solutions to this problem seem possible. The first is to choose one particular hierarchy in which all specific terms will be placed. For example, all named chemicals might be placed in a hierarchy based on Chemical constitution. All other hierarchies would list only groups of chemicals, and would stop just short of particular named chemicals. As a result, these hierarchies would classify only general references on these chemical groups; specific references to particular Polymers, Acids, Fermentation products, and so on would be in the Chemical constitution hierarchy.

This solution has two disadvantages. First, there are particular chemicals known only by trivial or trade names, which could not be assigned a place according to chemical constitution, and which would have to be placed in another hierarchy: *e.g.* gasoline in petroleum chemicals, Freon in refrigerants, protein in biosubstances. Second, search for all the references on a particular group—*e.g.* polymers—would retrieve only general references, none on specific polymers.

A second solution is therefore to place terms for specific chemicals in every hierarchy which literary warrant suggests. A reference to sulphuric acid might then be classed either in acids, petroleum chemicals, or sulphur compounds, according to its point of view—or in all three, if preferred. This solution aids generic search for groups of chemicals, but may readily lead to a scatter of information on individual chemicals.

A third solution is to represent all specific chemicals as a combination of their relevant attributes. Thus, aniline might be characterized as a basic, nitrogenous, benzene-derived, dye intermediate, toxic, etc., compound. In this solution, *all* hierarchies list only groups of chemicals, stopping short of particular named chemicals. This technique should only be used if the prime purpose of the index is generic survey. However, it is sometimes necessary for other reasons; as is discussed below.

COMPOUNDING ATTRIBUTES

The representation of a class by a compound of its attributes, to aid generic survey, has just been considered. There are circumstances when classes can be represented in no other way. For example, in Library Science we might formulate a provisional category as *library materials*. It would include such terms as pamphlet, photocopy, papyrus, Government publication, dictionary, French books, incunabula, first edition, etc. An attempt at logical division would reveal the presence of at least eight hierarchies, based on the characteristics of physical form, mode of inscription, base material, publisher, literary form, language, age, edition. Many other classes of library material could only be represented as a combination of these characteristics, *e.g.* Government pamphlets, French dictionaries. In such a case, the compounding of attributes is essential, using a schedule such as the following:

Library materials
  Physical form
    Shape
      Sheet
        Unfolded
          Broadsides
          Cuttings
        Rolled
        Folded
          Codex
            Pamphlet
            Book
      Tablet
  Method of inscription
    Manual (manuscripts)
    Mechanical
      Printed
      Duplicated
      Photocopied
        Reduced (microcopied)
  Base material
    Paper
    Papyrus
    Vellum
    Clay, etc.
  Indirect medium
    Projected
    Moving
    Magnified

Sense channel
  Visual
  Aural
  Tactile
Publisher
  Government
  Private
  Semi-published
  Unpublished (archive)
Mode of publication
  Serial
  Non-serial
Bibliographical form
  Bibliography, catalogue
  Reference book
    Dictionary, glossary, terminology
    Quotation, concordance, except
  Instruction, suggestion
    Law, Code, statute
    Agreement, treaty, contract
    Patent, standard, recipe
  Data book, tables
  Trade catalogues, exhibition catalogue
  Directory
  Statistics
  Thesis, dissertation
  Research report
  Imaginative work, etc.
Symbolical form
  Verbal text
  Non-verbal
    Diagram
    Map
    Picture
Script (Latin, Cyrillic, etc.)
Language
Age (*e.g.* Incunabula)
Edition

FAVOURED TERMS

There are several difficulties in the use of this technique. First, while a number of classes can be satisfactorily compounded in this way, some of the compounds may have become well-established and known by a single name. For example, the class of library materials which as to physical form is a rolled sheet, as to mode of inscription is photocopied, as to base material is a plastic, and as to mode of sensing is visual, is known as microfilm. The names for such established compounds must be listed in the facet.

This listing can be done in two ways. Either the class can be inserted in the schedule as a 'favoured' term, suppressing the fact of its compound origin, or it can be listed in the index to the schedule as a particularly frequently occurring example of a compound. The second method ensures that references to the class are found when a generic survey is made for one of its attributes—*e.g.* visual materials. This method is used in the Crop facet of the Colon classification, in which, say, wheat is listed as example no. 2 of a food-seed crop (food and seed being the compounded attributes).

INNUMERABLE ATTRIBUTES

The other difficulty of the technique of compounding attributes is in knowing when to stop. There are innumerable attributes by which a given class might be sought. To revert to an example in the last section, C. L. Bernier and K. F. Heumann[7] have suggested representing aniline as a six-carbon, seven-hydrogen, oily, combustible, etc., compound, as well as the five characteristics already cited. The technique may be of great value in a machine-sorting system designed primarily for generic survey, but to use it more than is essential in the ordinary special classification is unwise.

A moderate use of compounded attributes is found in an Aeronautics classification. In this we have a long schedule of aircraft structures. Any of these structures or their elements may be cross-classified by spatial attribute, so a set of adjectival attributes is provided, for compounding with any structural element. Examples follow:

46

Portion	Dimensions
Front, nose	Thin
Back, tail	Thick
Side	Tapered
Top	Low, deep
Bottom	High, tall
Tip	Arrangement
Shape	Vertical
Pointed	Horizontal
Twisted	Opposed
Triangular	Parallel
Square	In series
Concave	Eccentric
Notched	Symmetric
Bent	Asymmetric

N   *The functions of notation*

Once schedule order and its relation to combination and filing order have been established, a notation can be applied to the scheme. To do this requires understanding and decisions concerning five aspects of notation: its functions, the filing order of its functional parts, various techniques of establishing this order, the preferred attributes of the symbols used, and their allocation to the schedule.

Notation has three functions to perform. First, and most essential, it must be so designed that class numbers formed from it, and arranged ordinally, place the subjects in the preferred filing order. In other words, notation must mechanize arrangement.

Second, notation must be hospitable: that is, it must be possible to insert new terms, arrays, chains, hierarchies, or facets into the schedule in their preferred positions, and to give them a notational symbol which will correspond with that position and mechanize the arrangement.

Third, notation may, if required, reflect and demonstrate structural features of the subjects classified. There are two aspects of structure. The first concerns the structure of an individual compound heading: a class number may be designed to show the points at which combination of terms has occurred. In faceted classification, the display of such compound structure is essential, in order that the class number for each term in the compound may be free to extend (*i.e.* may be hospitable). The second aspect concerns the hierarchical structure in a facet: class numbers may be designed to show that two terms are in the same array, or the same chain, or the same hierarchy, or the same facet. This feature is not essential, and is not possessed by all notations.

Those which display this aspect of structure are called hierarchical, those which do not are non-hierarchical or purely ordinal.

The following sections of this guide attempt to set out some principles by which notation may be designed. It is not easy to describe this work briefly and simply, and special problems may arise which are not discussed. Notation is a mechanism to achieve certain ends—it is analogous to a machine—and in its design it is perhaps wise to seek the advice of an experienced practitioner.

O   *Functional parts and filing order*

To carry out the functions discussed above, notation in a special classification may need to have six or more distinct functional parts—*i.e.* groups of characters (numerals, letters, punctuation marks, etc.) performing specific functions. The main functional parts are listed below:
1. Characters (digits) for the scheduled terms in each facet.
2. Characters serving as facet indicators.
3. Characters for the literary form divisions—or a character serving as a form indicator.
4. Characters for relational terms.
5. A character for forming intra-facet compounds.
6. Characters for introducing class numbers from extraneous schedules (intercalation).

Not all notations need have all these parts. A purely ordinal notation may dispense with 2, 3, and 5. A classification which is self-sufficient can dispense with 6. Thus the only essential parts are 1 and 4—characters for scheduled terms and relational terms. In designing a notation the aim should be to have as few functional parts as is compatible with the work that the notation is asked to perform. However, since there are circumstances in which all the listed parts may be needed, the filing order of the whole set will be considered.

FILING ORDER

It is recommended that the characters for the various functional parts should have the following filing order:
Form indicator or characters
Relational terms indicator or characters
Facet indicators

Intra-facet connector
Intercalation starter
Scheduled terms
These functional parts will be explained and illustrated by the
following series of headings.

1. A	Library types	A
2. A2	Public	A22
3. A3	Non-public	A3
4. A32	Academic	A4
5. A321	School	A5
6. A322	College	A6
7. A329	University	A65
8. A33	Business	A7
9. A332	Industry	A8
10. A3322	Newspaper	A85
11. A333	Commerce	A9

12. A333	Commercial library	A9
13. A333B	Materials	A9B
14. A333Bm	report on	A9B.7
15. A333BC5	Storage	A9BC5
16. A333BC6	Cataloguing	A9BC6
17. A333BC6m	report on	A9BC6.7
18. A333BC6z4D32	Effect of staff shortage	A9BC6/D4
19. A333B (33)	Economics	A9B (33)
20. A333B22	Pamphlets	A9B3
21. A333B22C5	Storage	A9B3C5
22. A333B22–42	Government	A9B3–5
23. A333B22–42–52	French language	A9B3–5–7
24. A333B22–42–52–62	Bibliography	A9B3–5–7–9
25. A333B22–42–52–62 (33)	Economics	A9B3–5–7–9 (33)
26. A333B225	Sewn	A9B4
27. A333B52	French language	A9B7

The notation down the left-hand side is *hierarchical:* (*i*) All
terms in a given array differ only in the final digit—thus in subjects
5 to 7, numbers A321, A322 and A329 all come into the same
array. (*ii*) The successive terms in a chain differ only by the

addition of a right-hand digit—thus, A3, A32, A321. (*iii*) All terms in the library facet begin with the letter A.

The notation down the right-hand side is *ordinal* in that conditions (*i*) and (*ii*) above do not hold: digits have been assigned in the facet A simply to provide short ordinal numbers.

Both notations use numerals for scheduled terms and capitals as facet indicators. The capitals file before the numerals, so that subject 16 (cataloguing of materials in a commercial library) precedes 20 (a particular material, Pamphlets).

COMPARISON OF NOTATIONS

In subject 14 the hierarchical notation uses another set of characters, the small letters, for form divisions, whereas the ordinal notation uses numerals and a form indicator, the point. Both smalls and point file before capitals or numerals, so that subject 14 (a report on materials in a commercial library) comes before subjects 15 (storage of materials in commercial library) and 20 (pamphlets in commercial library).

In subject 18 the hierarchical notation uses the small z as a relational indicator, followed by a numeral to specify the relation, while the ordinal notation uses a stroke (using other punctuation symbols for other relations). The small z files after the other small letters used for form divisions, but before the capitals used as facet indicators. Similarly the stroke files between the point and capitals. Consequently subject 18 (effect of staff shortage on cataloguing) comes in the position shown.

In subjects 22 to 25 we have an example of a cross-classified facet. Materials can be arranged according to physical form (pamphlet), publisher (Government), language (French), form (bibliography), or subject (economics). The first hierarchy used is physical form. The ensuing hierarchies in the facet can be combined by an intra-facet connector, the dash. This files after the capitals, but before the numerals. Hence subject 22 (Government pamphlets) comes after 21 (storage of pamphlets) but before 26 (sewn pamphlets).

The last hierarchy in the materials facet, by subject, is directed to be obtained by intercalation from the UDC schedules. In subjects 19 and 25 the UDC number 33 for economics is used enclosed within brackets. The starter bracket files before the numerals, so that subject 19 (economics materials) comes before materials in special forms, languages, etc.

DISTINCT SPECIES OF CHARACTERS

The example discussed above has allocated a distinct species of character to each functional part of the notation, with the following filing order:

	Hierarchical	*Ordinal*
Form indicator	a to y	point
Relational indicator	z	stroke
Facet indicator	A to Z	A to Z
Intra-facet connector	dash	dash
Intercalation starter	bracket	bracket
Scheduled terms	1 to 9	1 to 9

This hierarchical notation represents the maximum degree of complexity as regards species of character, and results in complex class numbers which may not be easy to record or to remember. This multiplicity of characters is not essential. Alternative techniques for performing the same notational functions with simpler notations will be examined in the next section.

P *Alternative notational techniques*

One method of simplifying the complex hierarchical notation described in the last section has already been noted: the use of ordinal notation within a facet. A second method is hinted at by the use of z as a relational indicator. There is no need to use a new species of character (such as the stroke). A character in the existing species can be set aside to do the same work. This process can in fact be carried to its conclusion, and a complete ordinal notation can be produced from a single species, say, the capitals, thus:

Function	Characters used
Form divisions	A to C
Relational terms	D to F
Facet indicators	G to K
Intra-facet connector	L
Intercalation starter	M
Scheduled terms	N to Z

Thus subjects listed in the last section might have class numbers such as the following:

Subject	Previously cited numbers	New number
17	A333BC6m or A9BC6.7	GUHIRBB
22	A333B22–42 or A9B3–5	GUHOLQ
19	A333B (33) or A9B (33)	GUHM33

Such drastic simplification produces class numbers which are solid blocks of characters of a single species. The structure of the compound is in fact expressed, but it is not evident to the eye. Intermediate forms of simplification are possible in which the number of species is reduced, but not to unity.

RETRO-ACTIVE NOTATION

Facet indicators and an intra-facet connector can be eliminated
by the use of *retro-active* notation. In this, the schedule order must
be the reverse of combination order. The whole series of terms is
then numbered in a purely ordinal fashion with one species of
character, say the capitals, one condition being observed: for any
term, each successive character must be later in the alphabet than
the preceding character. A schedule such as the following results.

A	Form divisions, *e.g.*
AM	Report
B	Library administration, *e.g.*
C	Staff
CS	Shortage
D	Library processes, *e.g.*
DG	Storage
EF	Cataloguing
G	Library materials, *e.g.*
H	By subject
H (33)	Economics
I	By literary form, *e.g.*
IL	Bibliography
J	By language, *e.g.*
JR	French
K	By publisher, *e.g.*
KQ	Government
L	By physical form, *e.g.*
LP	Pamphlet
LT	Sewn
M	Library type
N	Public
P	Non-public
Q	Academic
R	Business
RT	Commerce

Previously cited subjects are now numbered as follows:

Subject	17	22	19
Class No.	RTGEFAM	RTLPKQ	RTH (33)

This retro-active notation also creates class numbers which are solid blocks of characters, but their structures—the points at which combination has occurred—are a little more evident: the letters in each scheduled term are of ascending ordinal value (RT, EF, AM, LP, KQ, etc.), and a join is signified by reversion to a letter earlier in the alphabet (T to G, G to E, F to A, etc.). Since the order of the alphabet is so well known, this structural feature can be readily recognized.

The use of retro-active notation instead of facet indicators can shorten the average length of class numbers—always a desirable aim—and elsewhere[9] I have examined conditions under which this is the case, and other means of achieving brevity.

Q   *The attributes of a good notation*

To be satisfactory, a notation must do more than perform the functions of mechanizing arrangement, displaying structure and allowing for expansion. It must also perform these functions elegantly, so as to be as little of a burden to the user as possible.

Perhaps the most important requirement of any notation intended for direct use by human beings is that the filing order of the characters employed should be immediately comprehensible to the user. The user is already trained to follow two conventionally used sequences—the letters of the alphabet and the numerals. If the notation uses letters *and* numerals, or uses other arbitrarily ordered signs such as punctuation marks, an element of hazard in the use of notation as a locating device is introduced, even though the amount of learning of the system which the user need undertake may, be small.

EASE OF RETENTION

The next most important feature of a notation is that it should be easy to retain mentally. Between the discovery of the class number and the finding of the actual reference there is a time-lag, which may be bridged by memory or copying. Easily retained notation may need no copying at all, while a complex symbol may be miscopied or the copy misread.

Ease of retention is greater for brief class numbers, and brevity is dependent on two factors: the length of the notational *base* (*i.e.* the total number of characters used in the notation), and the evenness with which digits are spaced out down the schedule.

Ease of retention is also greater for 'simple' class numbers than for 'complex'. It is not easy to define *simplicity*. The most obvious way in which a number may be simple is by the use of one species of character alone—letters or numerals. It is, however, by no means always certain that a concatenation of digits of one species—say, a solid block of letters—is the easiest to remember. E. J. Coates[8] suggests the following ranking for ease of retention.

1   One species with single separator : 33847(62148)
2   Ditto, using letter as separator   : 33847K62148
3   All one species   : 33847262148
4   Three species   : 3384U2k21P8

He prefers 1 to 2 since all species are not of the same psychological value as *separators*—if effective division of a symbol calls for a fresh species of character, the character chosen should have by convention a separating function, such as the punctuation marks, brackets, and strokes.

THE PSYCHOLOGY OF NOTATION

Unfortunately for the classifier, these various desirable attributes in notation to some extent conflict with one another: if only a single species of character is used—to have self-evident filing order—brevity is reduced and less memorable blocks of digits are formed. If maximum brevity is aimed at by using a long base with several species of character, self-evident filing order is lost and a complex class number results.

Since these desirable attributes of a notation—ease of recognition and retention—are psychological, and vary with the user and with his familiarity with the notation, it is not possible to lay down rules as to the best choice of characters for a notation. In deciding what base to use, and how to use it, the classifier should bear in mind the following points. First, who will most use the class numbers—the casual reader, or the classifier himself? Will the index users become very familiar with the numbers, or remain only distantly acquainted? Second, what level of complexity—in terms of complex class numbers and unfamiliar filing order—can these specified users be expected to cope with? The notation devised should be based on his answers to these questions.

R   *Allocation of numbers to terms*

Whatever other attributes a notation should have, everyone is agreed that the briefer the class number the better. The average symbol length can be reduced to its minimum if the length of each class number (or functional part of a class number) is inversely proportional to the frequency with which it is used. This axiom has been generally followed in hierarchical notation, on the assumption that the more general a term, the more frequent its use, and hence the shorter it should be.

Strictly hierarchical notation, with class numbers reflecting the hierarchy of terms, has to act on this assumption anyway, and makes no other attempt to achieve maximum brevity. In fact, it is not at all certain that the assumption is justified. In detailed indexing of papers and reports, the more general terms in a hierarchy may be rarely used. In a chain of classes, some of the intermediate terms may never be used as specific entries. Ordinal notation, breaking free from the need to reflect the hierarchy, can aim at allocating symbols to terms in direct relation to their frequency of use, so that a little-used general term may have a relatively long symbol.

In the allocation of numbers in an ordinal notation, this possibility should be constantly borne in mind. It may not be easy to obtain statistical information on the frequency of terms, and almost certainly the information available will not be sufficient to allocate symbols with anything like mathematical precision, but something can be done. Dale and Heumann have provided statistical information on the frequency of appearance of component parts of chemicals in a certain indexing system, which may be helpful in this particular field[10]. Krishna Rao has made a statistical study of the number of cultivated species in different groups of agricultural plants, useful in designing numbers for crops[11]. Other studies of this kind would be of value.

S *Classing with a faceted classification*

Anyone who has constructed a faceted classification will by then have such a good grasp of its structure that he will need little guidance on how to use it for classifying, but the main steps in the process may be given:

1. State the subject to be classified as a series of connected terms, thus:

   a. Relative costs of duplicating and photocopying (in Office Management).

   b. Extrusion coating of polythene on paper (in Container Manufacture).

   c. Effect of humus on crumb formation in loamy sand (in Soil Science).

2. Assign each term to its appropriate category in the classification, identifying it with a scheduled term, and assign the corresponding notational symbol.

	Subject term	Category	Scheduled term	Symbol
a.	Relative	Relation	Relation	5
	Costs	Admin. operatn.	Cost	de
	Duplicating	Machine	Duplicating	jr
	Photocopying	Machine	Photography	jrp
b.	Extrusion	Operation	Extrusion	Ffj
	Coating	Material	Coating	Dv
	Polythene	Product	Polythene film	Bu
	On	Relation	Relation	:
	Paper	Material	Coated paper	Dgl

c.	Effect	Relation	Effect	/
	Humus	Constituent	Humus	7i
	Crumb	Structure	Crumb	8m
	Formation	Process	Formation	5b
	Loamy Sand	Soil	Loamy Sand	9v

3. Assemble the notational symbols in the specified combination order:
   a. jrp5jrde
   b. BuDvFfj:Dgl
   c. 9v8m5b/7i

4. Construct reversed index entry from the class number:
   a. Cost: Duplicating: relative to: Photography
   b. Coated paper: Extrusion: Coating: Polythene film
   c. Humus: effect on: Formation: Crumb: Loamy sand

These reversed entries are often a valuable check on whether the classing has been accurate. If they fail to give the sense of the subject, the classing should be reconsidered.

5. Consider the derivation of added class entries. As originally developed, faceted schemes made only one entry in the classified catalogue for each subject, this has led to searching difficulties, and multiple class entry may be used.

For example, we can provide an added entry for subject *a* under Cost, de; for subject *b* under Coated paper, Dgl, and Extrusion, Ffj; and for subject *c* under Crumb, 8m.

These entries can be provided in two ways:
   (1) by dropping earlier symbols from the class number, to derive
       a. de (from jrp5jrde)
       c. 8m5b/7i (from Qv8m5b/7i)
   (2) by filing the whole of each class number at the added entry point, thus filing
       b. BuDvFfj:Dgl
   at Ffj and Dgl as well as at Bu.

T   *The alphabetical index*

Access to a classified catalogue must be by way of an alphabetical index, which is therefore its essential complement. To aid both the cataloguer and the user, we need first of all an alphabetical index to the schedules. This index should include (*i*) all single words and phrases used as class terms in the schedule, and (*ii*) cross-references from synonyms and from inversions of phrases. Thus the index to an aeronautics schedule includes the following entries:

Acrobatics, Km
Adiabatic flow, Ndh
Aerial photography, Add
Aerials, see Antenna, Wbi
Aeroembolism, see Decompression sickness, Ubi
Antenna, Wbi
Decompression sickness, Ubi
Flow, Nbf
Photography, aerial, see Aerial photography, Add

Where phrase inversion would lead to a repetition of the classified schedule in the index, as would the case for all the various types of Flow, only the main heading, Flow Nbf, is indexed.

ALPHABETICAL COMPLEMENT

The classified catalogue needs a further alphabetical complement: not only each scheduled term, but also those combinations of terms which have been used in the catalogue need to be indexed. The alphabetical index then displays groupings which are dispersed in the classified file.

The primary entry in the alphabetical file is the reversed index entry mentioned in section S, *e.g.*

Cost: Duplicating: relative to: Photography

This provides specific reference to the subject indexed. But a generic search, or simply a generic approach by the index user, requires that each subject be located if the sought heading in the alphabetical index is either (*i*) any one of the terms in the specific subject, or (*ii*) any term generic to one of these terms.

The first requirement can be met by inserting additional *rotated* entries in the alphabetical index, bringing each sought term to the front in turn, *e.g.*

Photography: Cost: relative to: Duplicating

Duplicating: relative to: Photography: Cost

(The term 'relative to' can be taken as unlikely to be sought.)

The second requirement is met by having an entry in the alphabetical index for each term in the schedules. Thus we have in the index all terms generic to those of the subject, *i.e.*

Administrative operations
Copying machines
Equipment
Finance
Machines

CHAIN PROCEDURE

Both requirements can also be met by the technique of *chain indexing*. The class number of a specific subject is laid out as follows:

9	Soils
v	Loamy sand
8	Structure
m	Crumb
5	Processes
b	Formation
/	effect
7	Constituents
	Chemical
	Organic
i	Humus

Index entries are constructed, starting with each term in turn, combining from bottom to top of the list, and neglecting redundant terms, thus:

Humus: effect on: Formation: Crumb: Loamy sand, 9v8m5b/7i (specific entry)

Organic constituents: effect on: Formation: Crumb: Loamy sand, 9v8m5b/7i

Chemical constituents: effect on: Formation: Crumb: Loamy sand, 9v8m5b/7b

Constituents: effect on: Formation: Crumb: Loamy sand, 9v8m5b/7

Formation: Crumb: Loamy sand, 9v8m5b

Processes: Crumb: Loamy sand, 9v8m5

Crumb: Loamy sand, 9v8m

Structure: Loamy sand, 9v8

Loamy sand, 9v

Sand, loamy, 9v

Soils, 9

In both the suggested methods of indexing, the generic terms will apply to more than one specific subject, and as the index grows the number of new generic terms or upper links in the chain to be added for each new subject will steadily decrease.

The problem of providing a complementary alphabetical index to the classified catalogue is not as straightforward as the above brief description might suggest, and the reader is advised to consult a book by E. J. Coates[12].

VERBAL HEADINGS

To facilitate the construction of chain index entries by purely clerical procedures, some care in the formulation of verbal headings in the schedules and their alphabetical index is necessary. For brevity and crispness in a classification schedule we might write:

Kv	Flying in unusual conditions
Kvb	Night
Kvd	Abnormal weather
Kvf	Over difficult terrain
Kvh	Ocean

Kvj	Mountain
Kvm	Desert
Kvp	Polar

Such a schedule relies on context for its interpretation. But if chain indexing is to be a clerical procedure, we cannot throw on the clerk the burden of deciding, for example, what should be the index entry if Kvm is encountered in a classified entry. In the classification schedule, each verbal heading must be in the form in which it is to appear in the chain index, thus:

Kv	Flying in unusual conditions
Kvb	Night flying
Kvd	Abnormal weather flying
Kvf	Flying over difficult terrain
Kvh	Ocean flying
Kvj	Mountain flying
Kvm	Desert flying
Kvp	Polar flying

The same is true for verbal headings which can appear in more than one context in a schedule. For example, in an aeronautics schedule, we may have Kj, Spinning, a flying operation, and Qef, Spinning, a method of mechanical working. The verbal headings should distinguish between the two, as follows:

K	Flying operations
Kh	Stalling
Ki	Diving
Kj	Spinning (flying operations)
Kp	Rolling (flying operations)
Qd	Mechanical working
Qdb	Forging
Qdf	Rolling (mechanical working)
Qef	Spinning (mechanical working)

These expanded verbal headings in the schedules should be carried over into the index to the schedules:

Abnormal weather flying, Kvd
Desert flying, Kvm
Diving, Ki
Flying operations, K
Flying over difficult terrain, Kvf

Forging, Qdb
Mechanical working, Qd
Mountain flying, Kvj
Night flying, Kvb
Ocean flying, Kvh
Polar flying, Kvp
Rolling (flying operations), Kp
Rolling (mechanical working), Qdf
Spinning (flying operations), Kj
Spinning (mechanical working), Qef
Stalling, Kh

U   *Mechanization*

The rotation of index entries, or the construction of a chain index, is a means of providing alphabetical access to a compound subject from every one of its terms. Other retrieval systems solve this problem in other ways. The UDC for example, provides only an alphabetical index to simple terms, but the compound class numbers can themselves be rotated.

Various mechanized systems are now available, such as hand-sorted or machine-sorted punched cards. These also use only an alphabetical code dictionary of simple terms, the mechanism giving access to each term or any combination of terms. There are circumstances when the use of such a mechanism may be more advantageous than the use of rotated or chain indexing—particularly when the typical subject catalogued contains many terms, all of which are useful in generic searches.

For a mechanized system, there is still value in constructing a faceted classification (although the coding will be different, since notations developed for a classified catalogue are not necessarily suited for a punched card system). The classification schedule, however, can serve three purposes: it can control the terms to be used in the code dictionary, it may guide the encoding of generic relations, and it may aid users in their choice of search terms.

Mechanized systems only alter the mechanics of retrieval, the physical operations by which a search is effected. They do not alter the basic problems of subject analysis. The structure of a subject field, as laid bare by facet analysis, remains the same, and the same classification schedule can be adapted to either card cataloguing or mechanized searching.

Most mechanized systems are post-coordinate. A faceted classification schedule and its alphabetical index can serve as a standard vocabulary for a post-coordinate system. Indexing proceeds as in the first 2 steps of section S. The entries in the alphabetical index and their contexts in the schedule help the indexer to decide when to use a "bound term" such as Polythene film, rather than both Polythene and Film. The index records (term cards, feature cards, punched cards, etc.) can be tagged with either the verbal term, such as Polythene film or the notational symbol Bu, or both, and filed either alphabetically or in symbol sequence.

Bibliography

Examples of faceted schemes are described in references 13, 17, 19 and 20, and these also indicate where complete schedules have been published.

1 *Library Association Record*, vol. 55, 1953, pp. 187–8.

2 The need for a faceted classification as the basis of all methods of information retrieval (UNESCO I.A.C. Doc. Ter. P.A.S. memo 320/5515), *Library Association Record*, vol. 57, 1955, pp. 262–8.

3 Bibliography of papers, *Journal of Documentation*, vol. 12, 1956, pp. 227–30.

4 Proceedings of the International Study Conference on Classification for Information Retrieval. London, Aslib, 1957.

5 *Classification Research Group Bulletin*, nos. 1–3, November 1956–June 1957 (out of print). No. 4 onwards, *Journal of Documentation*.

6 S. R. Ranganathan (a) *Prolegomena to library classification*. London, Library Association, 1957. (b) *Colon classification*, 5th ed. Madras, Madras Library Association; London, Blunt, 1957. (c) *Philosophy of library classification*. Copenhagen, Munksgaard, 1951.

7 C. L. Bernier and K. F. Heumann, Correlative indexes, III, *American Documentation*, vol. 8, 1957, pp. 211–20.

8 B. C. Vickery, Notational symbols in classifications, parts I–VI, *Journal of Documentation*, vol. 8, 1952, pp. 14–32; vol. 12, 1956, pp. 73–87; vol. 13, 1957, pp. 72–7; vol. 14, 1958, pp. 1–11; vol. 15, 1959, pp. 12–16.

9 E. J. Coates, Notation in classification, in ref. 4.

10 E. Dale *and* K. F. Heumann, *Statistical information on component parts of chemical compounds.* Washington, Chemical-Biological Coordination Center, March 1955.

11 D. B. Krishna Rao, *Facet analysis and depth classification of agriculture* (Ph.D. Thesis, University of Delhi, 1956).

12 E. J. Coates, *Subject catalogues; their headings and structure.* London, Library Association, 1960.

13 B. C. Vickery, *Classification and indexing in science,* 2nd ed. London, Butterworths, 1959.

14 S. R. Ranganathan, *Elements of library classification,* [2nd ed.], edited by B. I. Palmer. London, Association of Assistant Librarians, 1959.

15 Another account has been provided by B. C. Vickery, *Faceted classification schemes.* New Brunswick, Graduate School of Library Service, Rutgers the State University, 1966.

16 J. Mills, *The Universal Decimal Classification.* New Brunswick, Graduate School of Library Science, Rutgers the State University, 1964.

17 Four faceted schemes are described in the CRG Bulletin No. 7, *Journal of Documentation,* vol. 18, 1962, pp. 65–88; and others by C. A. Crossley in *Library Association Record,* vol. 65, 1963, pp. 51–9.

18 S. R. Ranganathan, Subject heading and facet analysis, *Journal of Documentation,* vol. 20, 1964, pp. 109–19.

19 D. J. Foskett, *Classification and indexing in the social sciences.* London, Butterworths, 1963.

20 *Classification of library science.* London, Aslib, for the CRG, 1965.

21 D. J. Foskett, Two notes on indexing techniques, *Journal of Documentation,* vol. 18, 1962, pp. 188–92.

22 D. J. Campbell, Making your own indexing system, *Aslib Proceedings,* vol. 15, 1963, pp. 282–303.

23 Jean Aitchison and others, Thesaurofacet, a thesaurus and faceted classification for engineering and related subjects. English Electric Co. Ltd., Leicester, 1969.

24 B. C. Vickery, *Techniques of information retrieval,* chapter 10. London, Butterworths, 1970.

25 Classification Research Group, *Classification and information control.* London, Library Association, 1969.

Index